A **SMITHSONIAN** COLORING BOOK

Kids'

Smithsonian Experience

Illustrations and Text by Stephen Kraft

Smithsonian Institution Press
Washington, D.C.

This coloring book was produced with
the advice and support of Kathy S.
Borrus and Norma Ryan of the
Smithsonian Museum Shops.

Introduction

Portraits and pandas, dolls and dinosaurs, airplanes and American Indians—these and other exhibits (and some of the buildings that house them) fill the pages of this coloring book. At any single time, at least two and a half million such attractions are on view in the 13 museums and the National Zoo which together compose the Smithsonian Institution. They range in age from fossils many millions of years old to works of art completed only yesterday. Many come as gifts, some are purchased, and some result from studies sponsored by the Smithsonian.

Turning the pages of this book—and coloring the drawings—will enable us to complete our very own album, and fix more clearly the memory of our visit to the Smithsonian.

In a number of the drawings, visitors themselves are shown walking toward and looking at the exhibits. Filling in these figures will add color and reality to the scenes. Since many of the museum buildings are made of a stone that is nearly white, coloring the clothing, as well as the grass, trees, clouds, and sky, will produce more complete and exciting pictures.

Carousel on the Mall Everyone loves to ride on a carousel—adults remembering the first days at a fair, children learning for the first time the pleasure of mounting a spirited pony and going round and round to the tune of sprightly band music.

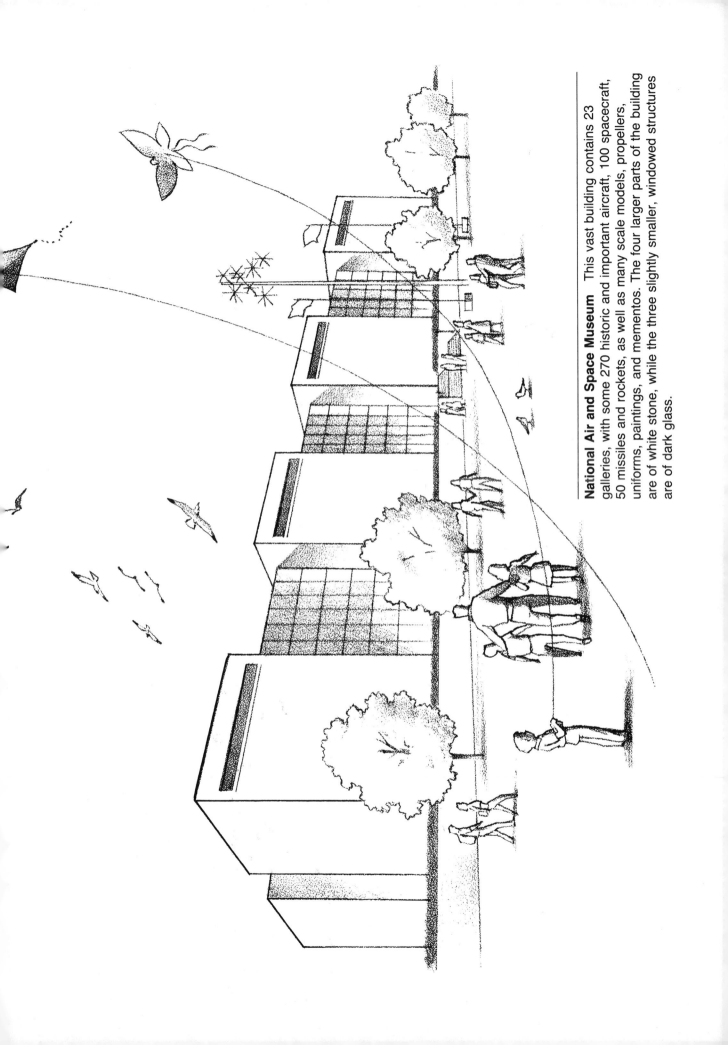

National Air and Space Museum This vast building contains 23 galleries, with some 270 historic and important aircraft, 100 spacecraft, 50 missiles and rockets, as well as many scale models, propellers, uniforms, paintings, and mementos. The four larger parts of the building are of white stone, while the three slightly smaller, windowed structures are of dark glass.

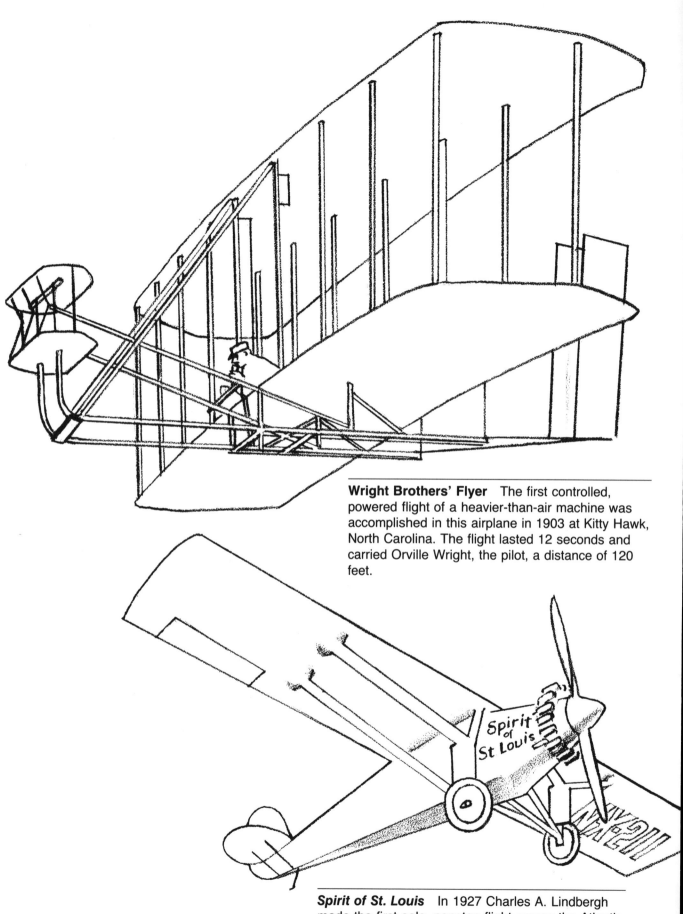

Wright Brothers' Flyer   The first controlled,
powered flight of a heavier-than-air machine was
accomplished in this airplane in 1903 at Kitty Hawk,
North Carolina. The flight lasted 12 seconds and
carried Orville Wright, the pilot, a distance of 120
feet.

Spirit of St. Louis   In 1927 Charles A. Lindbergh
made the first solo, nonstop flight across the Atlantic
Ocean, reaching Paris in 33½ hours. The fuselage,
wings, and tail of his airplane are silver in color,
while the engine housing is a light tan.

Columbia Space Shuttle Shown here as a small model—the tiny figures at lower left and right give an idea of its actual size—the shuttle is entirely white except for black and blue trim. The transporting vehicle is white and deep orange.

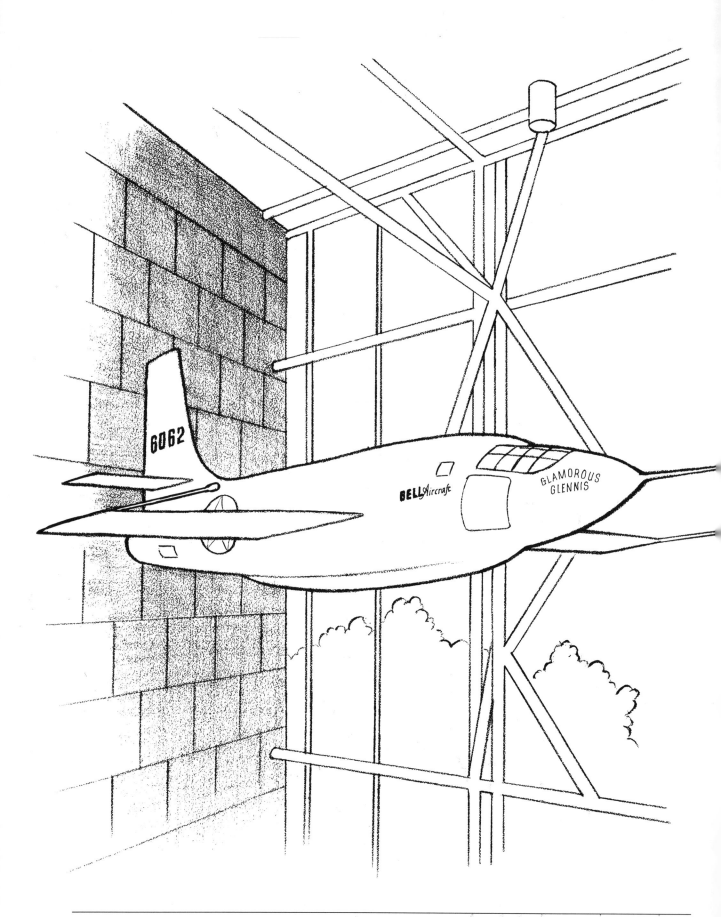

Bell X-1 In this airplane, Capt. Charles E. (Chuck) Yeager became the first pilot to fly faster than sound. The year was 1947. *Glamorous Glennis*, as it is known, made most of its flights not by taking off from the ground but by being carried aloft and launched from a B-29 bomber. Its greatest speed was about 957 miles per hour. The lower fuselage and wings are orange; the tail and top of the fuselage are white.

Montgolfier Balloon In 1783 two Frenchmen made the first long flight in a balloon filled with hot air. The size of the actual balloon—the National Air and Space Museum exhibits only a model—can be understood by noting the man in the gondola at the bottom. The balloon was colored blue, with yellow ornaments and red fabric drapery.

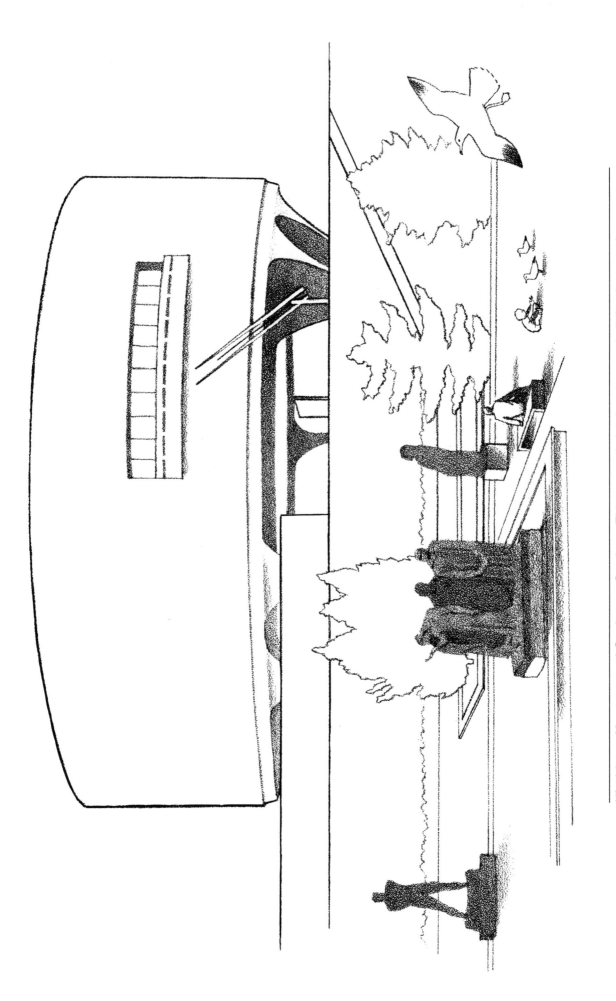

Hirshhorn Museum and Sculpture Garden This unusual circular concrete building houses the Hirshhorn collection of modern art. Displayed in the Sculpture Garden and on the plaza surrounding the museum are works by many different artists, both American and European.

Arts and Industries Building The second oldest of the Smithsonian buildings on the Mall, this is one of the few structures in the world with four identical sides. The bricks are deep red, with yellow and blue ornaments above and below the windows. The roof is blue-gray.

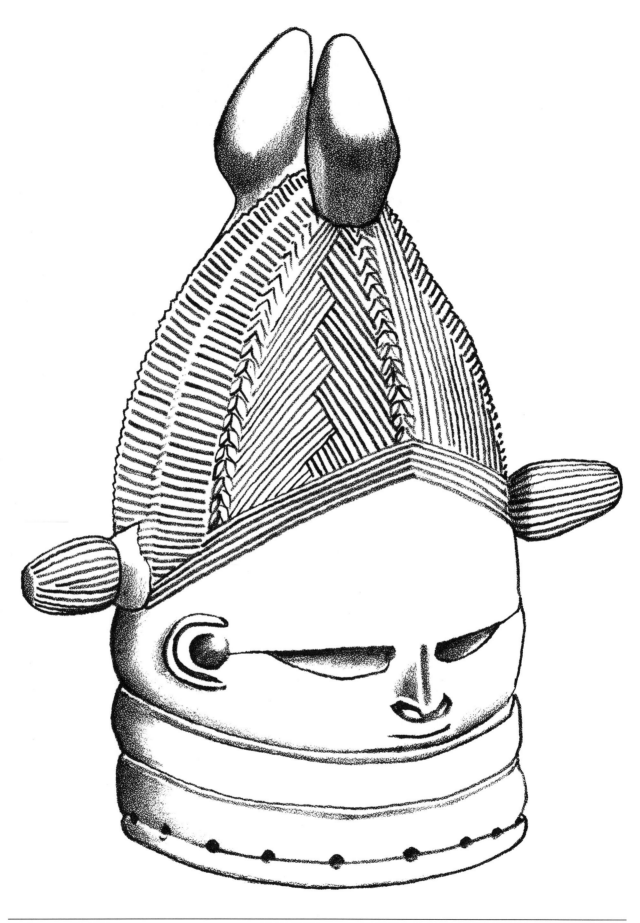

African Mask   A part of the collection of the National Museum of African Art, this wooden mask is worn during certain ceremonies by the Mende people of Sierra Leone, a country that lies a little north of the equator in western Africa. The mask is dark gray in color.

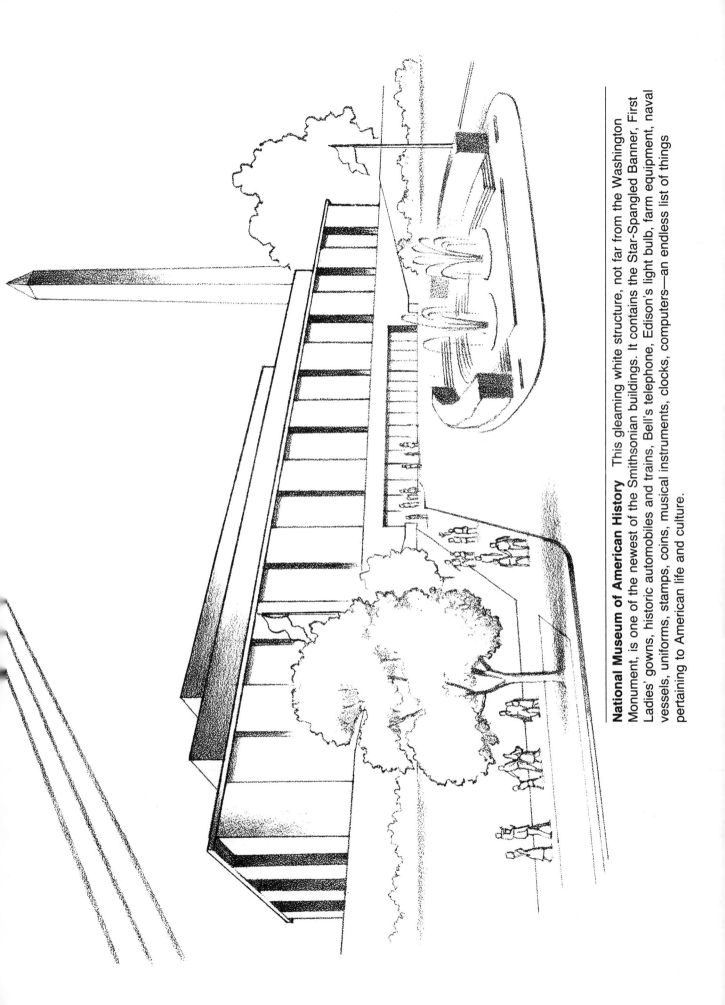

National Museum of American History This gleaming white structure, not far from the Washington Monument, is one of the newest of the Smithsonian buildings. It contains the Star-Spangled Banner, First Ladies' gowns, historic automobiles and trains, Bell's telephone, Edison's light bulb, farm equipment, naval vessels, uniforms, stamps, coins, musical instruments, clocks, computers—an endless list of things pertaining to American life and culture.

Star-Spangled Banner This is the flag that flew over Fort McHenry in Baltimore Harbor during an attack by a British fleet in 1814, and inspired Francis Scott Key to write the poem that later became the words of our National Anthem. The irregular line across the flag divides the original upper portion from the restored lower part. The light gray stripes are the ones to color red; the field in the upper left corner is dark blue with white stars.

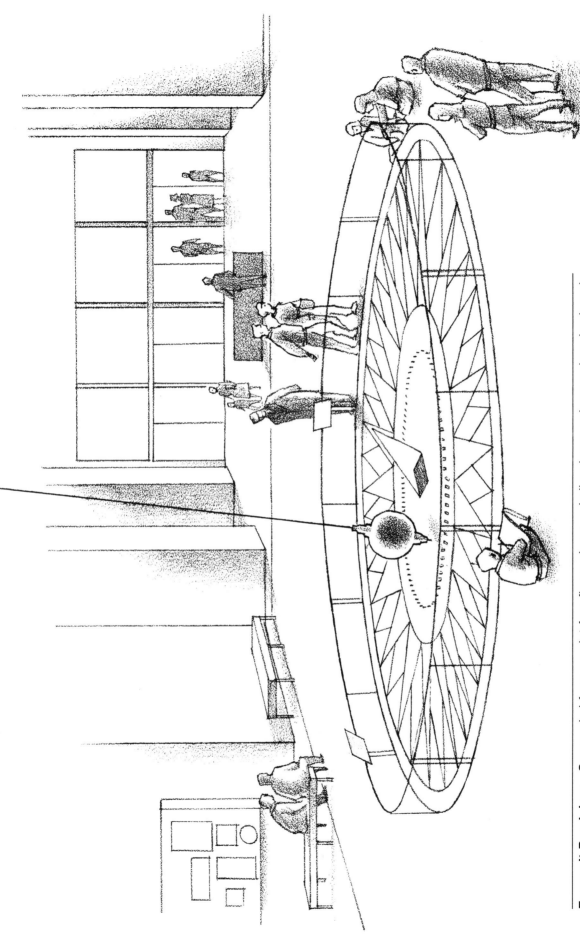

Foucault Pendulum Suspended from a point four floors above, a hollow brass sphere swings back and forth, its pointed tip knocking down, one by one, the red markers arranged in a circle around a compass rose inlaid into the floor. What actually rotates is not the pendulum but the floor, which rotates as part of the earth's surface. The pendulum is patterned on a device invented by a French physicist named Foucault.

Dolls' House The picture *below* shows a typical large American home of the early 1900s, when grandparents, parents, and children all lived under the same roof. Mr. and Mrs. Doll have 10 children. Also in the house are their nurse, a chambermaid, a cook, and a butler, as well as a number of dogs and cats. Most of the walls are papered, in a variety of colors and patterns. *Above* is the day nursery in this house. In the left corner stands the Doll family's own doll house. On the wall in the neighboring hall hangs a picture of a cat that used to live here. At the center, the twins are playing with their dolls and toy furniture. At the right are a book shelf, a hobby horse, and some trains, and in the corner is the house's present cat, lapping its milk.

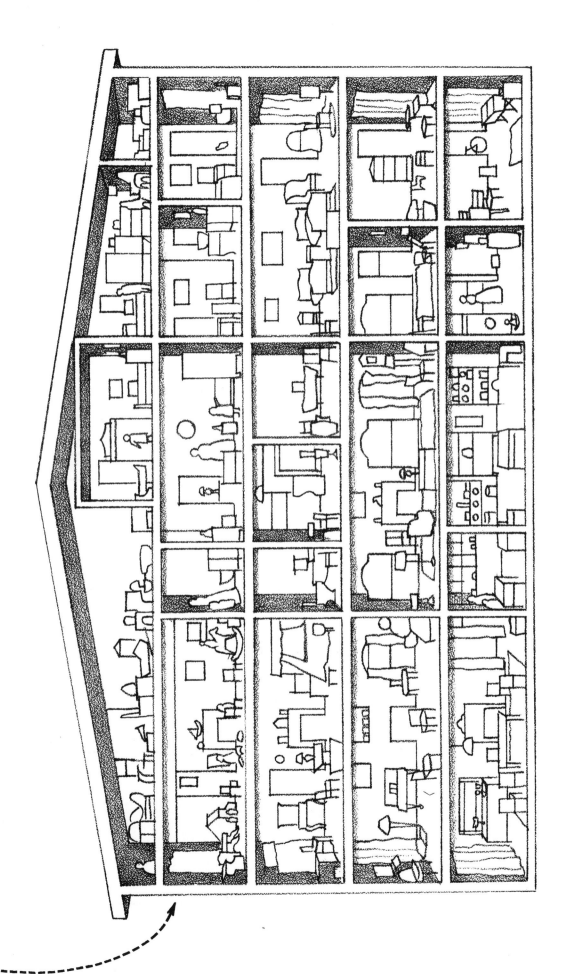

First Ladies' Gowns Models of the six most recent First Ladies are shown in a setting representing the Red Room of the White House. From left to right are Mrs. Reagan, Mrs. Carter, Mrs. Ford, Mrs. Nixon, Mrs. Johnson, and Mrs. Kennedy. The upper walls and draperies are deep red, as is the sofa. The lower part of the wall and the rug are an

Concord Coach This horse-drawn coach, built in 1848, met the railroad train. It was elaborately decorated in red and green.

Model T Touring Car About 15 million Model T Ford cars were built between 1908 and 1927. They were solid black inside and out, with fittings of brass.

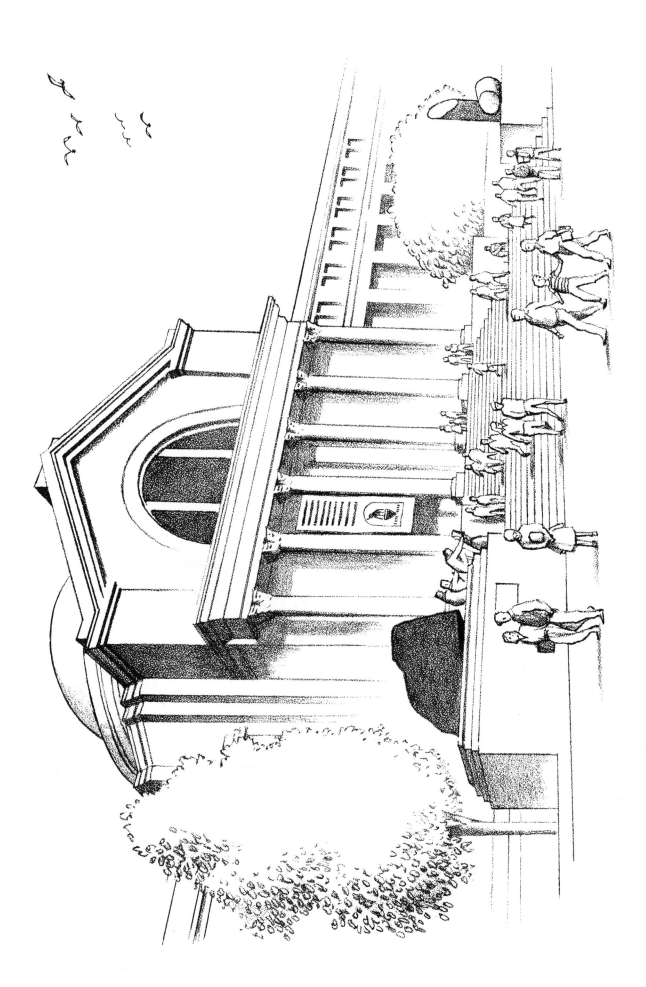

National Museum of Natural History This building contains an enormous variety of exhibits relating to human cultures, mammals, birds, amphibians and reptiles, fossils, sea life, insects, evolution, plants, meteorites, rocks and minerals, as well as a large collection of gems.

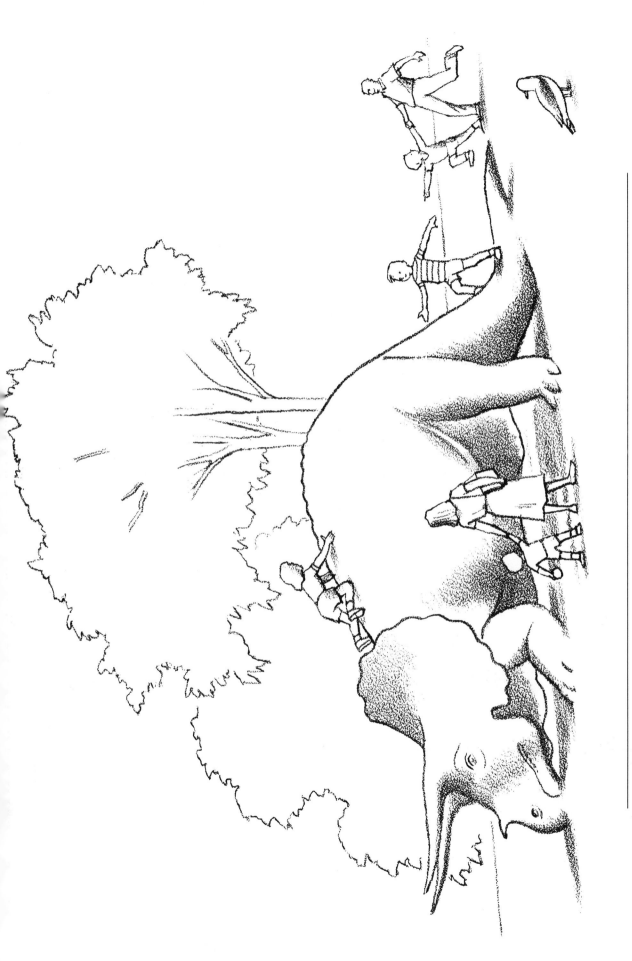

Uncle Beazley   Children love to climb on this 22-foot-long fiberglass replica of a Triceratops dinosaur, which stands on the Mall in front of the National Museum of Natural History, where skeletons of its cousins of long ago can be seen.

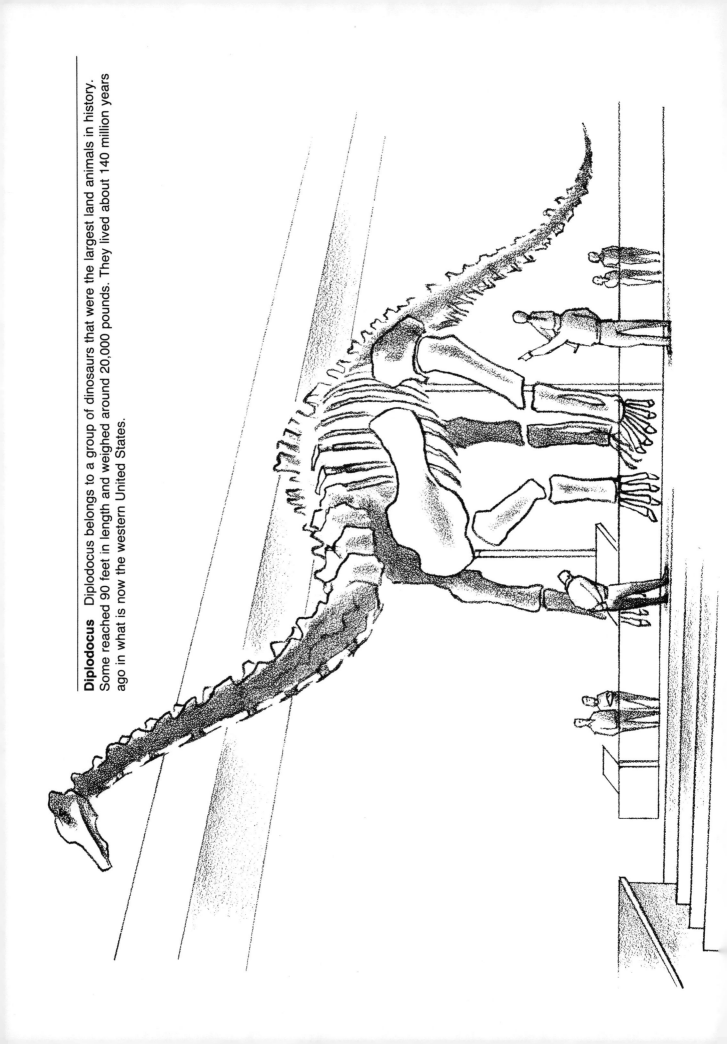

Diplodocus Diplodocus belongs to a group of dinosaurs that were the largest land animals in history. Some reached 90 feet in length and weighed around 20,000 pounds. They lived about 140 million years ago in what is now the western United States.

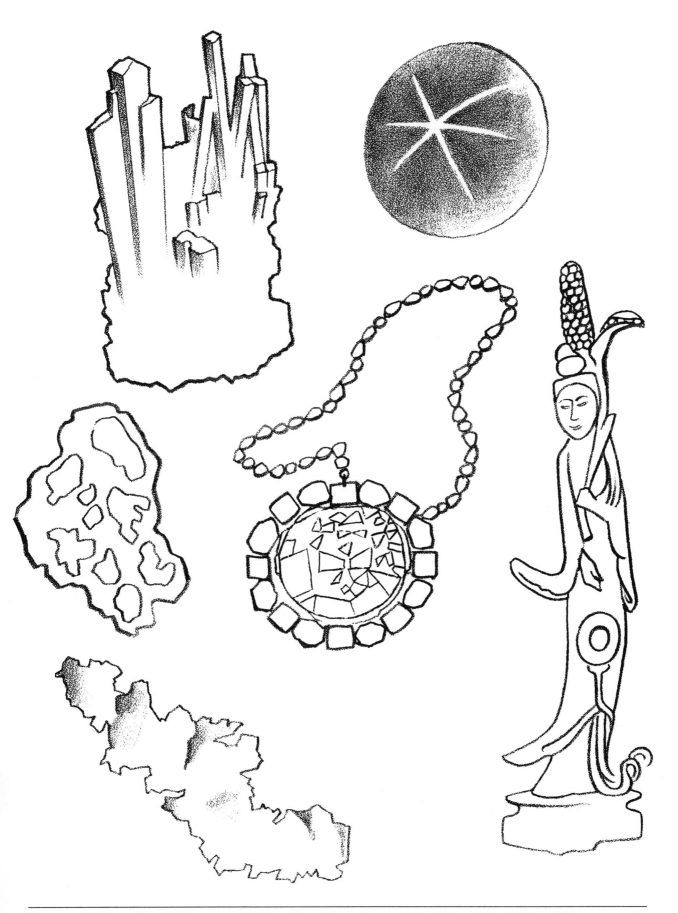

Gems and Minerals At the upper right is a deep blue star sapphire. Below it is a light red figure carved of coral. Next to that is a goldflake, then a many-colored piece of the mineral variscite, and a stibiconite crystal. At the center is the famous Hope Diamond, deep blue, surrounded by smaller, clear diamonds.

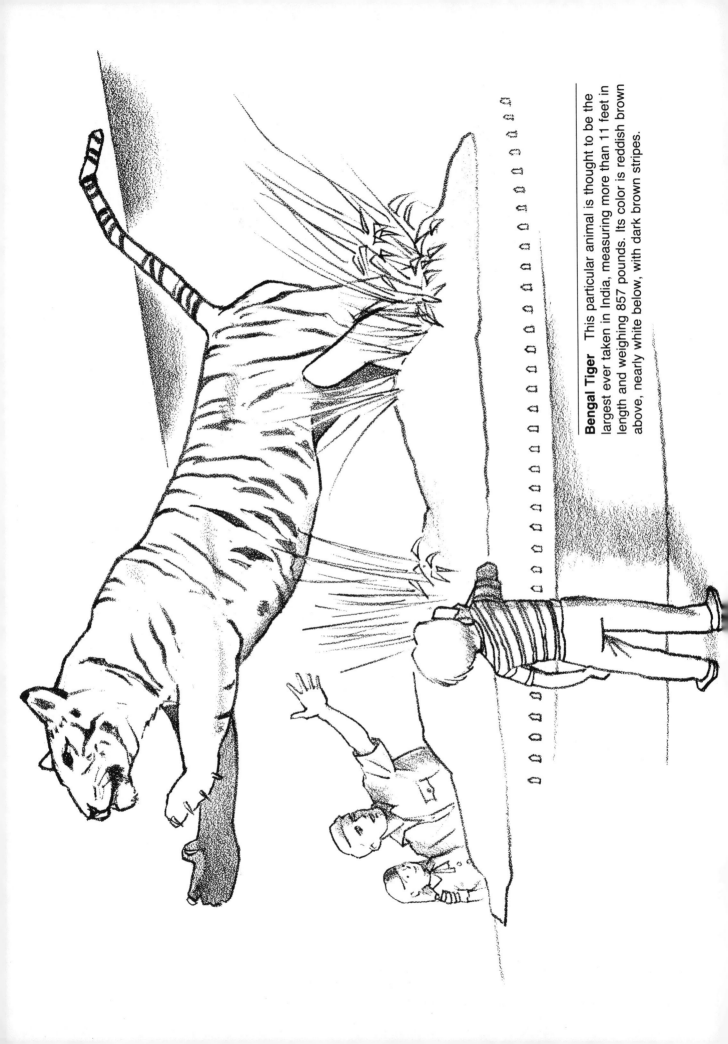

Bengal Tiger This particular animal is thought to be the largest ever taken in India, measuring more than 11 feet in length and weighing 857 pounds. Its color is reddish brown above, nearly white below, with dark brown stripes.

American Indians   This page shows a birchbark canoe from what is now the northeastern United States; a man in a ceremonial dress; an Eskimo about to launch a harpoon from his kayak; and two Indian women from the Southwest, one weaving on a large loom, the other decorating a clay pot.

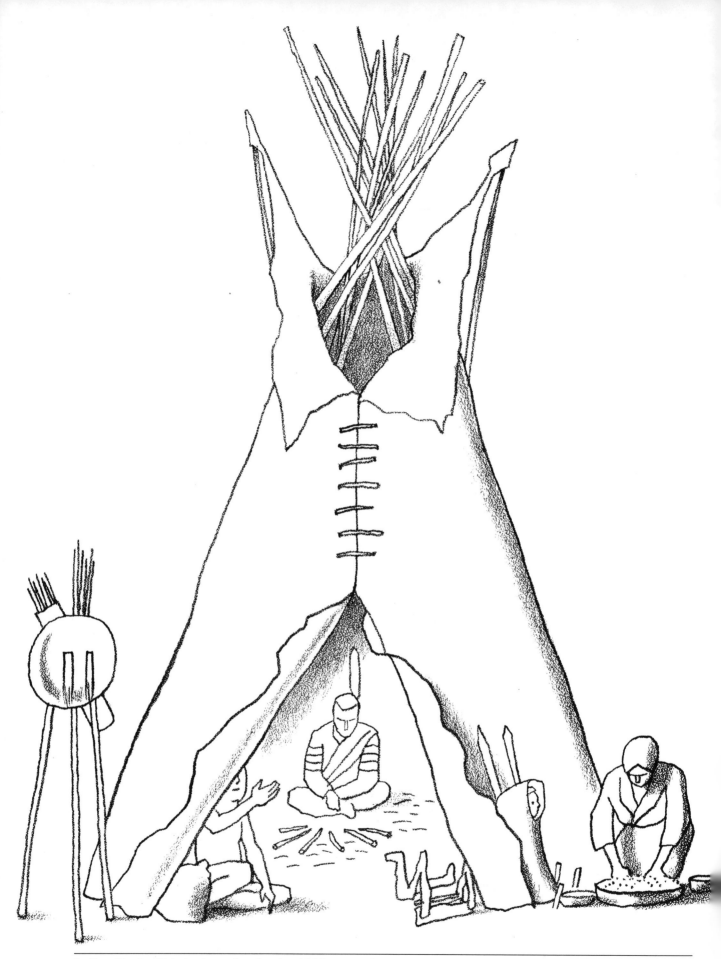

Indian Tent   This tent, made of animal hides, was large enough to shelter an entire family. It was supported by long poles that meet at the top, leaving a hole through which smoke from the fire inside the tent could escape. At the left is a stand holding a quiver full of arrows, while at the right we see an infant in its cradleboard next to its mother, who is kneading grain.

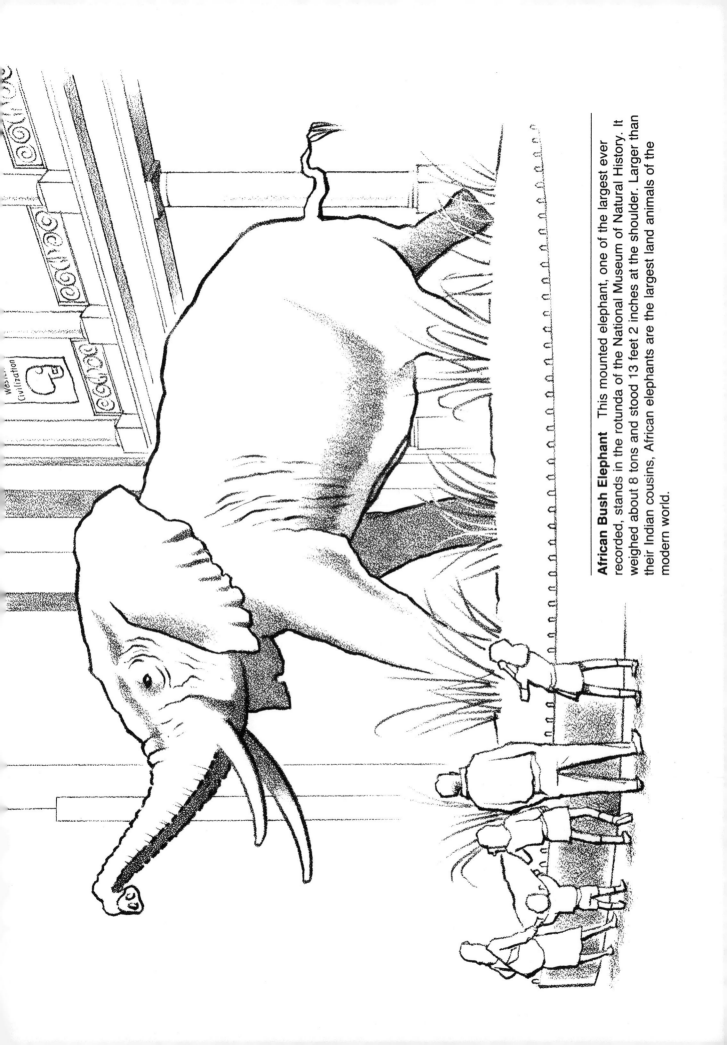

African Bush Elephant This mounted elephant, one of the largest ever recorded, stands in the rotunda of the National Museum of Natural History. It weighed about 8 tons and stood 13 feet 2 inches at the shoulder. Larger than their Indian cousins, African elephants are the largest land animals of the modern world.

National Museum of American Art Built almost one hundred and fifty years ago, and thus one of the oldest buildings in Washington, this large white structure contains more than 30,000 examples of American painting, sculpture, prints, and drawings from the 18th century to the present.

The Great Hall, National Portrait Gallery   This magnificent hall is two city blocks in length. Its floors are patterned in blue and gray, the columns are reddish brown, the walls are tan, white, and pale blue with gold ornaments. The glass dome at the center is blue in its outer parts and bright yellow at its center.

Old Patent Office Building Courtyard This enclosed area, shared by the National Museum of American Art and the National Portrait Gallery, can be entered directly from either of them. It contains two 100-year-old elm trees, as well as flower beds and sculpture. The fountain at the center and the Calder sculpture at the left are made of metal, and colored black.

The building that houses the Renwick Gallery was constructed during the Civil War period to serve as the original Corcoran Art Gallery, the first public art museum in Washington. Today the primary purpose of the Renwick is the exhibition of American design, crafts, and decorative arts. Its architect, James Renwick, who also designed the original Smithsonian "Castle," chose red brick for the outer surface. Among the rich ornaments are columns topped by capitals representing Indian corn.

Giant Pandas Ling-Ling and Hsing-Hsing arrived at the National Zoo in 1972 as a gift from the People's Republic of China to the American people. The green bamboo shoots on which we see one of the pandas dining form the largest part of the panda diet.